CW00400189

# Strength for Tomorrow

### Devotional Poems
written and illustrated
by B. Kaye Jones

Weston Hospicecare Ltd.
Branton House
21 Montpelier
Weston-super-Mare
Avon. BS23 2RJ
01934 625926

Kevin
Mayhew

First published in Great Britain in 1994 by
KEVIN MAYHEW LTD
Rattlesden
Bury St Edmunds
Suffolk IP30 0SZ


ISBN  0 86209 575 1
Catalogue No  1440340

© 1994 Kevin Mayhew Limited

Printed in Hong Kong
by Colorcraft

# CONTENTS

# Foreword

The first little book of my poems and paintings was compiled during a time of great uncertainty: I wasn't sure that I would survive the cancer that had traumatised my life.

'Trauma' is a much used word, but certainly describes the effect of cancer: there is a wound to the body, soul and emotions that needs help and healing from God.

Your suffering may not be the same as mine; it could be a bereavement, broken relationship or job-loss. Today all kinds of therapies are offered as problem-solvers, but not so much has been said about how the Christian faith can help us to come to terms with our particular trauma or wound – to find peace and help in our 'vale of tears' experience, by coming to a deeper relationship with Jesus Christ, through reading the Bible and prayer.

As time passed I began to realise, that with continuation of life and an improvement in health, there must come a help to face the future; to come to terms with living under the shadow of a life-threatening disease and to find the strength and grace to cope and even enjoy life fully again. So this book *Strength for Tomorrow* is about the grace for living, not dying; strength to carry on cheerfully, in spite of limitations. The indwelling power of Christ can and will meet our need, if only we ask him.

*'that you might walk ... strengthened with all might, according to his glorious power, unto all patience and long suffering with joyfulness, giving thanks unto the Father.'* COL. 1:10-12

B. KAYE JONES

*... My grace is sufficient for thee.*

2 Corinthians 12:9

# STRENGTH FOR TOMORROW

It was not easy learning how
to live 'just for today':
the path was sometimes difficult
with tears along the way.
I think I've grasped the lesson now
that you were teaching me –
although the future is unsure,
to live contentedly.

And for tomorrow's trial, you say,
there's full provision made:
of grace and strength; of hopefulness,
and joy that cannot fade.
Another lesson must be learned,
not only for today,
but for tomorrow I must trust;
Lord, take my fears away.

# Jesus, Lamb of God

Behold, the Lamb of God, who takes away all sin:
whose precious blood was shed for me,
to make me pure within.
I come now to that fountain – from sin I would be free –
and I wash me, wash me,
in the flood that flows from Calvary.

*… what are these which are arrayed in white robes …*
*these are they which came out of great tribulation and have*
*washed their robes, and made them white in the blood of the Lamb.*

REVELATIONS 7:13, 14

# HEARING GOD

I soften my heart before you, Lord,
letting go my own thoughts, my own will;
in faith drawing near, so your voice I can hear,
as my heart in your presence is still.

Then you speak words of guidance, of truth and of life
to the heart of this sinner forgiven;
your love filling my soul, cleansing, making me whole
as you draw me much closer to heaven.

*I will hear what God the Lord will speak.*

PSALM 85:8

# DESERT EXPERIENCE

I've been here to this desert land before,
a place that's desolate, and hard, and dry,
when all I am, and all I do, and feel
and know, must come into the ground and die;
this flesh, this self, this I –
deny – Lord.

This desert place is where I lose myself,
come to the end, abandon all to you.
I can't go on unless you take control
of all my life, I know you want me to
begin my life anew –
with you – Lord.

So here I stand today, my need exposed
by your great grace, to your all-seeing eye.
Forgive me, Lord, the self-strength, and the lack
of leaning hard on you; now hear my cry:
that I may learn to die –
this I – Lord.

*… except a corn of wheat fall into the ground and die,*
*it abideth alone; but if it die, it bringeth forth much fruit.*

JOHN 12:24

10

# ALABASTER BOX

Lord, I want my life to be, broken in its love for thee,
like the box of alabaster, broken for my Lord and Master,
in humility.

At thy feet, Lord, I would pour, all my heart's love,
more and more,
till the fragrance fills the air, with something lovely,
something rare,
and beautiful for thee.

But my love is poor and small, I would long to give my all,
rise above the human limits,
where my needy earth-bound soul sits,
chained by love of self.

Lord, my heart is open wide, take the self-will and the pride,
hindrances that come between, and deep resistances unseen
unknown to all but thee.

Something beautiful for thee; how I long that others see,
only thy love flowing through, only thee in all I do –
my Jesus glorified.

'And behold, a woman of the city, who was a sinner... brought an
alabaster box of ointment, and stood... at his feet
behind him weeping, and began to wash his feet with tears...
and anointed them with the ointment...

LUKE 7:37-38

13

# A Prayer for my Grandchildren

When they are grown,
and you have called me home,
may they remember me –
not for my words or actions,
or seeming piety –
but for the love I bore them;
your love, Lord, shining through.
O grant my prayer, that they in turn
may love and serve you, too.

*My little children, let us not love in word,
neither in tongue; but in deed and in truth.*

1 John 3:18

# CHILDREN

Babies, soft and round and warm,
innocent of face.
Little girls a-partying, all pink bows and lace.
Small and grubby boys aglow, recounting breathlessly
what fun they had, what wonders seen,
whilst fishing in the sea.
Children, children, big and small,
precious gifts of love,
rare and costly treasures sent
from Father-God above.

*Lo, children are a heritage of the Lord:*
*and the fruit of the womb is his reward.*

PSALM 127:3

# REST

Anxious and angry,
here I am depressed,
wond'ring and fretting
when I should just rest.
I cannot change my lot at all
by worrying or fear –
then, in my negativity
a still, small voice I hear.

Tenderly speaking
(he who knows me best)
'Come to your Saviour,
I will give you rest;
and take no thought about your life,
nor of tomorrow's trial –
O weary, heavy-laden one,
just come and rest a while.'

*Come unto me, all ye that labour and are heavy laden,
and I will give you rest.*

MATTHEW 11:28

# CONFIDENCE

I have no confidence unless
I find myself within your care;
no strength to stand and 'hold my own',
no courage to go here or there;
but when I wait on you, I find
that I can walk, that I can run
and by your mighty power, I fly
on eagle's wings towards the sky.

*He giveth power to the faint, and to them that have no might,*
*he increaseth strength ... they that wait upon the Lord shall*
*renew their strength: they shall mount up with wings*
*as eagles; they shall run and not be weary, and they*
*shall walk, and not faint.*

ISAIAH 40:29, 31

# POWER OF CHOICE

For this day I choose life, Lord,
I choose you;
and by that choice receive
a different view:
my introspective, unbelieving thoughts
just fall away –
with joy and thankfulness
I face today.

*… I have set before you life and death, blessing and cursing:*
*therefore choose life, that both thou and thy seed shall*
*live … that thou mayest love the Lord thy God,*
*for he is thy life, and the length of thy days.*

DEUTERONOMY 30:19, 20

# The Overcomer

O Lord, who overcame the curse of sin and death,
submitting to the Father's will,
rejecting love of this world and of self
and thus enduring suffering, until
you paid that all-atoning price of sacrifice
and died upon a cross of shame –
help me lay down my will, my self, my all
and be an overcomer through your name.

*The next day John seeth Jesus coming unto him,
and saith, 'Behold the Lamb of God,
which taketh away the sin of the world.'*

John 1:29

# Refreshment

Come and fill my life with your love, O Living Stream;
Everlasting Water, spring up, spring up in me.
Floods upon a dry ground, of desert and of drought –
come, refresh my emptiness, banish fearful doubt.

*... but the water that I shall give him,*
*shall be in him a well of water,*
*springing up into everlasting life.*

JOHN 4:14

# His Love

You loved me when I was unformed –
your word has told me so;
through days of careless youth, your love
I didn't fully know.
My present sins I cannot hide
and yet you draw me to your side,
with love so true, so vast, so wide,
you love me.

You loved me when I turned away,
and lived so selfishly;
and as I struggled to return
you loved me tenderly.
You loved me then, you love me now,
and one day you will show me how
you love me, love me through eternity.

*… I have loved thee with an
everlasting love: therefore with loving kindness
have I drawn thee.*

JEREMIAH 31:3

# SUFFERING

People ask me 'Tell me why,
(if there is a God on high)
you should suffer as you do?
There are many others, too,
suffering anguish, pain or grief,
needing comfort and relief.'
And I answer 'I don't know
why I have to suffer so:
one day God will make it plain.
I can only say again –
others' pain to me is real,
others' suffering I can feel
with a deeper empathy,
and a kinder sympathy;
I can offer them my hand,
telling them – I understand.'

*Blessed be ... the God of all comfort;*
*who comforteth us in all our tribulation, that we may be*
*able to comfort them which are in any trouble,*
*by the comfort wherewith we are comforted of God.*

2 CORINTHIANS 1:3 (B)-4

# A BLESSING

May God's blessing be always your portion,
may his love in your heart never dim,
may each step that you take know his guidance,
and your life bear much fruit for him.

*He that abideth in me, and I in him,*
*the same bringeth forth much fruit:*
*for without me ye can do nothing.*

JOHN 15:5

# Village Churches

In many country villages
the old, grey churches stand,
so picturesque and comforting,
the churches of our land.
We visit and enjoy them;
they are our heritage,
and in the book for visitors
we sign the crowded page.
We look around admiringly –
'tis part of holiday –
we whisper, read and walk about –
but seldom kneel to pray
or feel his presence there. O may
our churches never be
old halls where once we worshipped God –
just monuments to see.

*… for mine house shall be called a
house of prayer for all people.*

ISAIAH 56:7

29

# BITTERNESS

There dropped into my mind, like thistledown,
a tiny seed of bitterness, which I
did cherish and attend to carefully;
a seed that later could become a tree –
of bitterness.

I started to rake up old wrongs and hurts
and watered well with tears of unbelief;
by dismal thoughts of uselessness and need,
I helped to nourish well that little seed –
of bitterness.

We have an enemy, who, cleverly,
in some sore trial can tempt our saddened hearts
to contemplate the past and present pain
and resurrect some buried hurt again –
to bitterness.

I saw his plan, his deadly strategy,
and grasped that root and tore it from my heart
by praying 'I forgive, I let it go,
I will not let that seed of evil grow –
to bitterness.'

*… lest any man fail of the grace of God;
lest any root of bitterness springing up trouble you,
and thereby many be defiled.*

Hebrews 12:15

31

# HAVE FAITH IN GOD

When doubt and darkness fill your mind
– have faith in God.
When others' actions are unkind
– have faith in God.
When days are wearisome and long,
when strength is gone, and fear is strong –
then let this be your battle-song:
'Have faith in God'.

*... Jesus saith unto them, 'Have faith in God.'*

MARK 11:22